We find the amazing in the ordinary everyday with lists, polls and quizzes. Helping us to appreciate, in fun and quirky ways, the world in which we live.

Creating interactive content, R Amazing! is a safe place to explore different topics and share your views.

It is ok to disagree with us regarding who or what we think is amazing! We share our thoughts on our website and in our books to enable debate and discussion.

We encourage the expression of opinions in an appropriate way with an understanding that it is ok for people to have differing views.

R Amazing! debates should be conducted politely and respectfully, ending with an agreement and common ground, even if that is to agree to disagree.

www.r-amazing.com

People R Amazing
By Mark 'Markus' Baker & Adam Galvin

Published by R-and-Q.com.

ISBN: 978-0-9933275-1-3

PLEASE NOTE:

From our point of view, the people in this book are shown because we think they are amazing!

With regards to each person on this list, it is assumed, our expectation and belief that each individual does NOT endorse, support or are linked to the R Amazing brand in any way. That is until, and most importantly if, each of the individuals, or their representatives, ever state otherwise. Until such a time they are NOT endorsing, supporting or linked to R Amazing in any way.

Written by Adam Galvin
Illustrated by Markus Baker

As I gazed into the sky, a night star caught my eye
It spoke to me of dreams...
It said:
Dare to dream
Big, bold & colourful dreams
For dreams hold no boundaries
No Limits
Never let go of your dreams
And your dreams will never let go of you
So dare to dream

For one day your dream will become you!

"

*What would you
attempt to do...*

...if you knew you could not fail?

Robert H. Schuller

LEARN MORE AT
www.r-amazing.com/keller/

Helen Keller

At the age of one and a half, Helen Keller was extremely ill and lost both her vision and hearing. She overcame the adversity of being blind and deaf during her remarkable life, standing as a powerful example of how determination, hard work, and imagination can allow an individual to triumph over hard times. By overcoming difficult conditions with a great deal of persistence, she grew into a respected and world-renowned activist and author.

Although the world is full of suffering, it is also full of the overcoming of it.

LEARN MORE AT
www.r-amazing.com/edison/

Thomas Edison

Thomas Edison was not always successful, as a young boy, he often got into trouble at school. His teacher called him, "addled" which means slow or dim. Thomas Edison is most famous for his invention of the light bulb; however, success was not instant. In fact, it took Edison thousands of attempts. When a newspaper reporter asked Thomas Edison how he felt about his 10,000 failures, Edison replied:

> *I have not failed 10,000 times. I have not failed once. I have succeeded in proving that those 10,000 ways will not work. When I have eliminated the ways that will not work, I will find the way that will work.*

*The sky's the limit.
Go for it!*

Instead of saying...

I have failed

Ask...

What have I learnt from this?

What do I need to do next?

LEARN MORE AT
www.r-amazing.com/stutzman/

Matt Stutzman

Matt Stutzman was born without arms – just stumps at the shoulders – but there is nothing he cannot do. He had to learn to do everything a person might normally do with one's arms, but amazingly with his feet. He can drive a car without any special modifications – by using his right foot on the steering wheel, and can even write with both feet, both shoulders, and even his mouth.

He holds a world record for the most accurate distance shot in archery, *which* includes able-bodied archers.

You have to do it. You have to follow your dreams. You've got to go after it.

Instead of saying...
I can't do this
Say...
I can't do this yet!
In time I will be able to do it!

*Everybody has
a unique gift.*

LEARN MORE AT
www.r-amazing.com/curie/

Marie Curie

Marie Curie's contribution towards the fight against cancer is remembered because of her discovery of radium and polonium treatment. Curie was the first woman to make such a significant contribution in the field of science, she flourished as a scientist because of her ability to observe, deduce and predict. She was awarded two Nobel Prizes, as well as being the first woman to be awarded a place in the Pantheon. Named in honour of her, Marie Curie is a charity which provides care and support for the terminally ill and their families.

> *Life is not easy for any of us. But what of that? We must have perseverance and above all confidence in ourselves. We must believe that we are gifted for something and that this thing must be attained.*

LEARN MORE AT
www.r-amazing.com/branson/

Richard Branson

It is a success that was never expected for a dyslexic, near-sighted boy. In fact, school was a nightmare for Richard, he was embarrassed by his dyslexia as he had to memorize and recite word for word in public.

"You've got one go in life, so make the most of it." was the advice of Richard Branson's Grandmother. Those words go right to the heart of his belief in making it on his own, leading to him heading over 150 enterprises that carry the Virgin brand name. It is estimated that Branson's personal wealth is nearly £2.4 billion.

Holding the record as the fastest to cross the Atlantic Ocean by boat, he has followed that personal dream and made the most of life.

Do not be embarrassed by your failures, learn from them and start again.

Nothing is impossible when you put your mind to it!

Instead of thinking...
I'll never be that smart.
Think...
I am learning how to do this!
It may take a little time and effort!

P
A A
41
LEARN MORE AT
www.r-amazing.com/bannister/
3:59.4

Roger Bannister

In 1954, Roger Bannister, a 25-year-old British medical student, made history by becoming the first man to run a mile in less than four minutes. A feat that was thought to be humanly impossible!

His time was 3mins 59.4 seconds, achieved at the Iffley Road track in Oxford and watched by around 3,000 spectators.

Roger's approach to record-breaking was to break up the four minutes: four laps each completed in just under one minute!

> *The man who can drive himself further once the effort gets painful is the man who will win.*

Instead of thinking...

That's impossible...

Think...

I know someone who can do it!

I will learn from them.

*Believe in yourself...
believe in your dream!*

LEARN MORE AT
www.r-amazing.com/pankhurst/

Emmeline Pankhurst

Emily Pankhurst played a militant role in helping gain women's right to vote. Through the political action of the WSPU (Women's Social and Political Union), she led a group of passionate women, who were willing to take drastic action. The group were responsible for launching demonstrations, smashing windows and tying themselves to railings. Many of the members were arrested. In 1928, Emily Pankhurst's passionate belief that women deserved equal rights became a reality and women were granted equal voting rights with men.

> *Once determined, nothing on earth and nothing in heaven will make women give way.*

LEARN MORE AT
www.r-amazing.com/gandhi/

Mahatma Gandhi

Mahatma, meaning "great-souled", is fondly remembered by the world as one of the most famous freedom fighters in the history of mankind. Leading India in its struggle for freedom against British rule, he taught Indians how to stand up for their rights in a non-violent way.

India received independence on 15th August 1947.

> *You are but the products of your thoughts; what you think, you become.*

When you put your mind to it you can be anything you want to be.

Instead of thinking...
I give up...
Think...
I'll use a different strategy.

LEARN MORE AT
www.r-amazing.com/pele/
7

Pele

During the 1958 World Cup, the 17-year-old Pele scored a staggering 6 goals leading the Brazilian National Team to victory. Consequently, Brazil won its first World Cup that year. The world paid attention to the young star – Pele.

Things weren't always good for Pele; he grew up in poverty. To help his family financially he used to polish shoes. Growing up, Pele showed a great interest in soccer, displaying a great talent. He was playing for a local minor league club when he got his first break.

Success is no accident. It is hard work, perseverance, learning, studying, sacrifice and most of all, love of what you are doing or learning to do.

Instead of thinking...
I can't get any better...
Think...
I'm always improving!

Imagine...Believe...Achieve.

E=MC2
LEARN MORE AT
www.r-amazing.com/einstein/

Albert Einstein

Probably known as the most famous and accomplished scientist of all time, Albert Einstein's image can be recognised around the globe. However, Einstein was not always considered a genius. He got poor marks during his school years.

Over the years, Albert Einstein has been awarded many scientific prizes for his works, notably the Nobel Prize for Physics in 1921. He came up with his now famous E = MC2 equation.

*You never fail until you give up,
until you stop trying.*

*Trust in your ability…
believe in yourself!*

Instead of thinking...

I made a mistake...

Think...

Mistakes help me improve!

What have I learnt?

LEARN MORE AT
www.r-amazing.com/rowling/
HP

J.K. Rowling

From living on state benefits, J.K Rowling became a multi-millionaire within just a few years. She is the United kingdom's best-selling living author.

The idea for the Harry Potter series was created on a delayed train from Manchester to London in 1990. The first book in the series, Harry Potter and the Philosopher's Stone, was completed in 1997.

Harry Potter was initially turned down many times, however, that did not stop J.K.Rowling, she went on to become one of the greatest children's books ever, selling more than 400 million copies worldwide!

It is impossible to live without failing at something, unless you live so cautiously that you might as well not have lived at all - in which case, you fail by default.

Instead of thinking...

Right or wrong ...

Think...

Options.

*Hard work...
Perseverance...
Determination.*

LEARN MORE AT
www.r-amazing.com/paula/

P A A
101
2:15:25

Paula Radcliffe

Paula Radcliffe is a former world champion in the marathon, half marathon and cross country. She believes in hard work, determination and not setting herself limits in order to achieve her goals and ambitions in life. Some of her achievements are a three-time winner of the London marathon, three-time New York Marathon champion, as well as winning the 2002 Chicago Marathon.

In 2003 Paula Radcliffe became the fastest women's marathon runner ever. With a world record time of 2 hours 15 minutes and 25 seconds.

> *Never set limits, go after your dreams, don't be afraid to push the boundaries. And laugh a lot, it's good for you!*

*Once you start your
journey do not stop!*

Instead of thinking...
What could go wrong...
Think...
What could go right!

LEARN MORE AT
www.r-amazing.com/oprah/

Oprah Winfrey

Born in rural poverty, Oprah's mother raised her dependent upon government welfare payments to survive. The Oprah Winfrey Show was the highest rating television programme, dubbing Oprah as the "queen of media" and was broadcast from 1986 to 2011.

By the age of 32, she'd become a millionaire and has been ranked the richest African-American of the 20th century.

President Barack Obama presented Oprah with the Presidential Medal of Freedom, which is the Nation's highest civilian honour.

Doing the best at this moment puts you in the best place for the next moment.

LEARN MORE AT
www.r-amazing.com/flo/

Florence Nightingale

Thanks to Florence Nightingale, much of what we know about clean and organised hospitals has come from her teachings. In particular, she is famous for her work during the Crimean War, whereby she changed the face of nursing from an untrained profession to a highly skilled and respected profession.

I attribute my success to this: I never gave or took any excuse.

Instead of thinking...

I can't do this in one go...

Think...

I can do it one step at a time.

Close your eyes. Imagination can take you anywhere you want. You just have to believe.

LEARN MORE AT
www.r-amazing.com /qe1/

Queen Elizabeth The first

Considered by many as the greatest monarch in English history, Elizabeth became queen in 1558 at the age of 25 and was known to be quick-witted, clever, as well as being ruthless and calculating as any king before her. Unfortunately, she inherited a bankrupt nation, with opposing religions, making England a less powerful country than France and Spain. Many were not convinced of her ability and believed that she needed to marry quickly, relying on a husband for support. However, Elizabeth had other ideas! She was committed to preserving English peace and stability. As a ruler, she was ahead of her time in her understanding of public relations, and her popularity remained undimmed.

If we still advise we shall never do.

LEARN MORE AT
www.r-amazing.com/walt/

Walt Disney

The name Walt Disney is easily recognised by lots of children around the world. However, it was not always that way. He started his own company, known as Laugh-O-gram, to create his own short animations. Although the cartoons were popular, he had to close the company. This was not going to stop Walt Disney!

Once again he opened another company. Unfortunately, Universal studios gained control. Once again Walt Disney had to start over again. After lots of failures, he never gave up on his dream!

All our dreams can come true if we have the courage to pursue them.

The difference between winning and losing is most often not quitting.
Walt Disney

Instead of thinking...

This is going to
be too challenging...

Think...

It is going to be worth
all the extra effort!

LEARN MORE AT
www.r-amazing.com/rosa/

Rosa Parks

In 1955 Rosa Parks helped initiate the civil rights movement in the United States when she refused to give up her seat to a white man on a bus. The day Rosa Parks was tried and convicted of violating the segregation laws, the leaders of the local black community organised a bus boycott, which lasted more than a year. During the boycott, the U.S. Supreme court ruled that the bus segregation was unconstitutional. Consequently, Rosa Parks has become recognised as a symbol of dignity and strength to end racial segregation.

I have learned over the years that when one's mind is made up, this diminishes fear; knowing what must be done does away with fear.

LEARN MORE AT
www.r-amazing.com/churchill/

Winston Churchill

Famous for his inspiring and motivating speeches, dogged determination and refusal to give in. Winston Churchill was Britain's prime minister for most of World War II.

Known for his 'V for victory' sign, Churchill led Britain through the Blitz, as well as the Battle of Britain.

Success is walking from failure to failure with no loss of enthusiasm.

Instead of saying...

I'm making lots of mistakes, I'm no good at this...

Say...

Good, I'm making mistakes, this shows I'm having a go and learning!

The only thing you should doubt are your limits!

LEARN MORE AT
www.r-amazing.com/amelia/

Amelia Earhart

Flying solo across the Atlantic, Amelia Earhart was given the U.S. Distinguished Flying Cross for being the first female to set this record. She was an American aviation pioneer, as well as becoming a bestselling author. She used her fame to promote two causes that were very important to her: the advancement of women, as well as the advancement of commercial aviation. During an attempt to circumnavigate the globe she suddenly disappeared, never to be seen again.

> *The most difficult thing is the decision to act, the rest is merely tenacity. The fears are paper tigers. You can do anything you decide to do. You can act to change and control your life; and the procedure, the process is its own reward.*

LEARN MORE AT
www.r-amazing.com/obama/

Barack Obama

Barack Obama is best known for being the first African American President of the United States.

On January 20, 2009, Barack Obama became President. His journey began in 1996 when he decided to enter the world of politics. Throughout his political career, he has been recognised as being an excellent speaker. It took Obama 13 years to achieve his dream.

'Quit' isn't in my vocabulary!

Instead of saying...

I don't know...

Say...

I don't know yet!

LEARN MORE AT
www.r-amazing.com/val/

Valentina Tereshkova

A former textile worker, the then 26-year-old Valentina Tereshkova from the Soviet Union, became the first woman in space. Her journey into space was seen to be a clear signal in the development of equal rights for women. She stated, "On Earth, men and women are taking the same risks... Why shouldn't we be taking the same risks in space?"

On June 16, 1963, the space shuttle was launched, amazingly circling the globe a total of 48 times!

A bird cannot fly with one wing only. Human space flight cannot develop any further without the active participation of women.

PAA
LEARN MORE AT
www.r-amazing.com/ali/

Muhammad Ali

Larger than life, Muhammad Ali was first famous for his boxing, celebrated for his style and witty pre-fight talk. His other causes, such as social and political campaigning transformed him into one of the most iconic stars on the planet.

In 1969 Muhammad Ali refused to serve in the military due to his religious beliefs. He was stripped of his championship title, fined $10,000 and sentenced to five years in prison. However, he did not serve his time and his conviction was overturned.

In 1974 Ali entered the ring as a 3-to-1 underdog to fight for the Heavyweight Championship dubbed, "The Rumble in the Jungle". In round eight, Ali prevailed knocking the Champion to the canvas!

> *If your dreams don't scare you, they aren't big enough.*

Instead of saying...

I have had enough...

Say...

Great things take time!

Win or learn, always give 100%

LEARN MORE AT
www.r-amazing.com/malala/

Malala Yousafzai

Whilst travelling home from school in 2012 a gunman shot Malala Yousafzai for defying the Taliban, who demanded that girls should not be allowed to receive an education. Miraculously, she survived and has continued to speak out about the importance of education for girls. In 2013 Malala was nominated for a Nobel Prize. The following year, she was once again nominated, and this time won, becoming the youngest person to receive the Nobel Peace Prize! Malala, in 2017, became the youngest-ever UN Messenger of Peace and started her studies in Philosophy, Politics and Economics at Oxford University.

> *Education is education. We should learn everything and then choose which path to follow.*

LEARN MORE AT
www.r-amazing.com/lee/

Bruce Lee

Known as the most famous martial artist of the 21st century, Bruce Lee was also an actor, filmmaker and revolutionary thinker, Lee created his own martial arts style called 'Jeet Kune Do' meaning 'The way of the intercepting fist.'

School didn't interest Bruce. Before his 18th birthday, his mother paid for him to travel to America, to avoid getting into trouble and claim his dual citizenship.

Bruce Lee became an international star when his films became box-office sensations in Asia and later Hollywood. Enter the Dragon is considered one of the greatest martial arts movies of all time.

Defeat is a state of mind; no one is ever defeated until defeat has been accepted as a reality.

My picture of the most amazing person in the world!

The most amazing person in the world is

....

I love it when this amazing person...

....

....

....

....

....

This person is amazing because...

....

....

....

....

MORE BOOKS BY R&Q

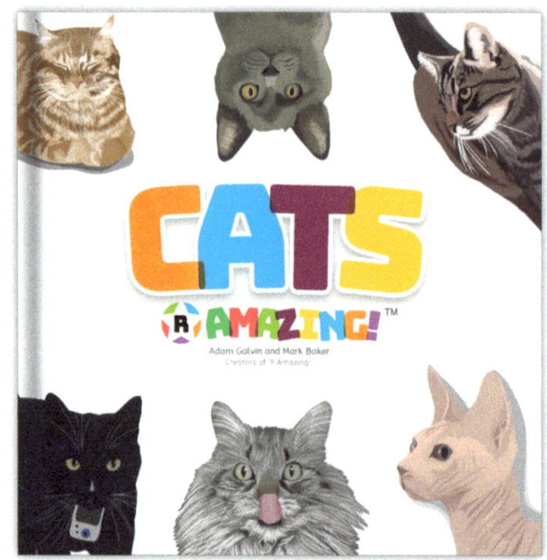

check out the books and merchandise at

w w w . R - a n d - Q . c o m